READ AND SHARE
ANYWHERE!

Bookmobile
Fountaindale Public Library
Bolingbrook, IL
(630) 759-2102

By Gwen Ellis

Illustrated by Steve Smallman

Tommy NELSON

Published in Nashville, Tennessee, by Thomas Nelson. Thomas Nelson is a registered trademark of HarperCollins Christian Publishing, Inc.

Scripture quotations are taken from the International Children's Bible®. © 1986, 1988, 1999, 2015 by Thomas Nelson. Used by permission.

Stories retold by Gwen Ellis

Illustrations by Steve Smallman

Works by Gwen Ellis © 2008, used by permission.

Works by June Ford © 2008, used by permission.

Works by Laura Minchew © 2008, used by permission.

The Library of Congress Cataloging-in-Publication Data

Ellis, Gwen.
[Our together-time Bible]
Read and share devotional / Gwen Ellis ; illustrations by Steve Smallman and Jeffrey Ebbeler.
p. cm.
Originally published: Our together-time Bible. Nashville, Tenn. : Thomas Nelson, c2008.
Includes indexes.
ISBN 978-1-4003-1717-2 (hardcover)
1. Bible stories, English. 2. Christian children—Prayers and devotions. I. Smallman, Steve. II. Ebbeler, Jeffrey. III. Title.
BS551.3.E545 2010
220.9'505—dc22 2010048856

Mfr.: DSC / Shenzhen, China / June 2019 / PO# 9530207

ISBN 978-1-4002-1207-1

Printed in China
19 20 21 22 23 / DSC / 5 4 3 2 1

Dear Parents,

Spending quality time together with your family is easy and fun with this book of 75 classic Bible stories. Even on the go, you can create memories while helping your children discover more about God and His Word and growing your faith together as a family.

Each Bible story section contains a beloved Bible story, "Read and Share Together" questions that will inspire deeper conversation and more thoughtful responses to the Bible story, and a prayer.

My prayer is that even during our busy lives that are full to bursting some days that you and your family will begin a tradition of time together that will bring joy into your lives long past the conclusion of this book.

Blessings,
Gwen Ellis

TIPS

- Choose one Bible story a week to read and discuss with your children or class. The more you create fun and lively discussions, the more your children will respond, listen, and look forward to your next time together.

- Read the stories, questions, and prayers in a memorable way. Then encourage your children to act out the Bible scenes using different voices for different characters.

- Involve older children as readers.

- Encourage children to talk about the topic during meal-time, drive time, etc., throughout the week.

- Have each child think of ways that the topic relates to his or her life, and then encourage the child to apply it.

- Create fun activities (which may include playing games, creating crafts, baking, or discussing the topic) sometime during the week.

CONTENTS

New Testament Stories

GOD MADE THEM ALL

Genesis 1

In the beginning God made heaven and earth. Then God said, "Let there be light." God called it day. He called the darkness night. God divided the air from the water. Then God made puddles and oceans and lakes and waterfalls and rivers. Next

Read and Share Together

What are some things God made?
What did God say about everything He made?

He said, "Let there be plants. Let there be a sun in the sky during the day and a moon and stars in the sky at night." God made the seasons, too, and it was good. God said, "Let there be living things in the oceans. Let there be birds in the sky. Let there be animals on earth." And every time God said, "Let there be . . ." it happened!

Prayer

Dear Lord, thank You for making our beautiful world
and all the animals, birds, and fish. Thank You for
the sun and the moon and the stars too. Amen.

ADAM AND EVE

Genesis 2:7–9, 15–22; 3:20

God named the first man Adam. God put Adam in a beautiful garden. He gave him all the animals. He gave him all the fish and the birds too. Then God gave Adam one more thing. God made

Read and Share Together

Where did Adam and Eve live?
What did God give Adam?

a woman to be Adam's wife so he would not be alone. Adam named his wife Eve. God made both Adam and Eve like Himself. On day seven God rested from all His work. And God said it was all "Good!"

Prayer

Dear Lord, thank You for creating a beautiful world for Your people to live in and for loving us so much that You give us family and friends to share Your world with. Amen.

THE SNEAKY SNAKE

Genesis 2:16–17; 3:1–6

God gave Adam and Eve one rule. "Eat anything you like except the fruit from the tree in the middle of the garden." A sneaky old snake came to Eve. "Eat it, then you'll know everything, just

Read and Share Together

What animal tricked Adam and Eve?
What is it called when we disobey God?

like God." So Eve ate the fruit and gave some to Adam. And he ate it too. Adam and Eve disobeyed God, and this is called sin. Because of sin, Adam and Eve faced consequences.

Prayer

Dear Lord, please help me to obey You always.
Please help me to say no to sin because I want
to obey You all the days of my life. Amen.

OUT OF THE GARDEN

Genesis 3:8–24

One evening God came to visit Adam and Eve. But they were hiding. When God found them, He asked, "What have you

Read and Share Together

Why were Adam and Eve hiding from God?
How did God feel about what Adam and Eve did?

done?" Adam told God everything. God was sad. Because they had disobeyed God, Adam and Eve had to leave the beautiful garden. When they were outside of the garden, Adam and Eve had to work very hard to grow food.

Prayer

Dear Lord, I do not want to make You sad.
Please help me never to hide from You and
always obey Your commands. Amen.

NOAH'S ARK

Genesis 7:1–4, 12; 8:1–19

God told Noah to build a boat, sometimes called Noah's ark. Then he told Noah to fill the ark with his family and two of every animal. Noah obeyed God. It rained for forty days and forty nights. After the rain, there was still water everywhere! Everyone and every creature on that ark practiced patience as they waited for the day to come when they could leave the boat. One day

Read and Share Together

Why did God want Noah to build a boat?
What kind of bird did Noah send out to find dry land?

Noah went to the top of the boat and opened the window he had made. He sent a dove out to see if it could find dry land. If it did, they could get off the boat. The bird came back because it couldn't find a dry place to land. Noah waited seven days and sent the dove out again. This time it came back with a green leaf in its mouth. He waited seven more days and sent the bird out again, and this time it did not come back. Noah knew that meant the dove had found a safe home, because the water on the ground was drying up. Soon Noah and his family could get off the boat. Their waiting would be over.

Prayer

Dear Lord, You watched over Noah, his family, and the animals during the Great Flood. Thank You for watching over me now just like You watched over Noah. Amen.

THE RAINBOW

Genesis 8:18–22; 9:1–17

When everyone was out of the boat, Noah built an altar. He thanked God for keeping them safe. Then something wonderful

Read and Share Together

Why did God put a rainbow in the sky after the Great Flood?
What did God promise?

happened! God put a beautiful rainbow in the sky and made Noah a promise. "It will never flood over the whole earth like that again," God said. When God makes a promise, He keeps it.

Prayer

Dear Lord, thank You for sending us beautiful rainbows
in the sky to remind us of Your promises. Thank You
for keeping all Your promises in the Bible. Amen.

BABEL

Genesis 11:1–9

Many years later there were lots of people on the earth. They all spoke the same language. Some people who lived in the city of Babel became too proud. "Let's build a tower that reaches

Read and Share Together

What city became too proud?
What happened to the people who
were building the tower?

to the sky. We'll be famous." God caused them to speak different languages so they couldn't talk to one another. Because they couldn't understand one another, they stopped building the tower.

Prayer

Dear Lord, You are the one true God. Thank You for helping me to understand and respect how great You are. Amen.

PROMISED LAND

Genesis 12:1–9

God told Abram to move to a new place. Abram had no map. God said, "I will show you where to go." Abram started out walking. He took his wife, nephew, and servants with him. When

Read and Share Together

Whom did Abram take with him on his journey?
What new land did Abram travel to?

Abram and his family got to a land called Canaan, God said, "This is your new home. I am giving it to you and to everyone who will ever be in your family."

Prayer

Dear Lord, help me learn to trust You just like Abram did, no matter where You are leading me. Amen.

THE ANGRY BROTHER

Genesis 25:27–34; 27:1–37, 43–44

Esau and Jacob were brothers. Esau was the oldest, which meant when their father's property was divided, Esau would get the most. It was called his "birthright." One day Jacob made soup while his brother, Esau, went hunting. When Esau came home, he was very, very hungry. "Let me eat some of that soup,"

Read and Share Together

What did Jacob cook?
Why did Esau get angry with Jacob?

Esau said. "I'll trade you some soup for your birthright," Jacob answered. Foolishly, Esau agreed to the trade. Their father gave Esau's birthright to Jacob. Later, Esau thought, *That trade was a big mistake. My birthright is worth more than a bowl of soup!* Esau became very angry. His anger made Jacob afraid. Jacob went far away to his uncle's house, and Jacob did not come home for a long time.

Prayer

Dear Lord, when I am angry, help me to remember to calm down and think about what I'm doing and saying. Amen.

JOSEPH'S COAT

Genesis 37:3, 12–28

Jacob gave Joseph a beautiful coat with long sleeves. This made his brothers jealous. One day Jacob said, "Joseph, go check on your brothers." So off Joseph went. His brothers saw him coming. "Here comes the dreamer," they said. "Let's get rid of him." The brothers hated Joseph. But one of them said, "Let's not hurt him. Let's just throw him down this well." He planned to rescue Joseph later. So they took off Joseph's coat and

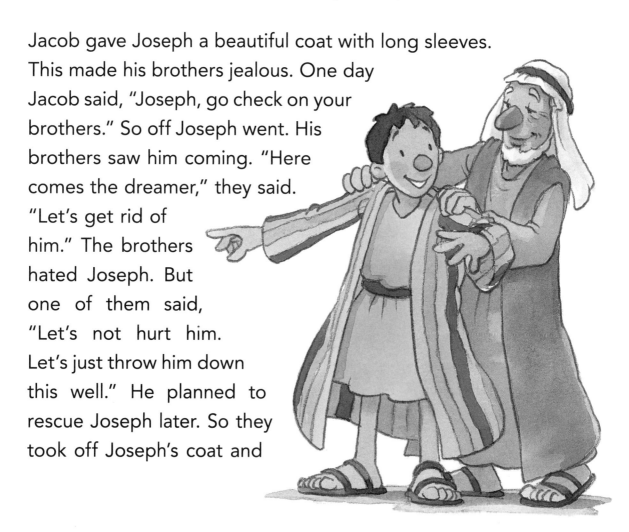

Read and Share Together

Who gave Joseph his beautiful coat?
What did Joseph's brothers do to him?

threw him in. About that time, some men on camels rode by. "Hey," the brothers said, "let's sell him to be a slave." They sold their own brother.

Prayer

Dear Lord, when I am jealous, please help me to see that You have blessed all of Your children in special ways and with special gifts. Amen.

BABY MOSES

Exodus 2:3–10

The kind of Egypt made a law that said Israelite baby boys must be thrown in the river. But an Israelite woman decided to hide her baby from the evil king. So she got a basket and fixed it so the water could not get inside. Then she put the baby into the basket and put the basket into the river. The baby's big sister,

Read and Share Together

Why did the mother want to hide her baby?
Who found baby Moses and named him?

Miriam, stayed close by to see what would happen. God was watching over the baby. When the princess came to the river to take a bath, she saw the basket. "Go get that basket," she told her servant. The princess looked inside the basket. Just then the baby cried, and she felt sorry for him. The princess decided to keep him as her son. She named him Moses.

Prayer

Dear Lord, thank You for always watching over
me and saving me from evil. Amen.

MOSES AND THE BURNING BUSH

Exodus 2:11–3:12

Moses was raised as a prince of Egypt. But when he was grown up, Moses did something very bad. He killed another man. Moses ran away to live in the desert. He married a lady named Zipporah. One day when Moses was out with the sheep, he saw a bush in the desert. It was on fire, but it didn't burn up. Moses went to look at this strange fire. God spoke to Moses from the fire. "Don't come any closer. Take off your sandals. You are on holy ground." Moses was scared. He covered

Read and Share Together

What did Moses see while watching his sheep?
What did God ask Moses to do with His people?

his face. "Go, bring My people out of Egypt," God said. "I can't do that," Moses said. But God promised to help Moses lead the people.

Prayer

Dear Lord, thank You for helping me all the time, especially when You ask me to do hard things. Amen.

THE KING SAYS NO

Exodus 4:29–5:9

God's people, the Israelites, were slaves in Egypt. When the Israelites heard that God had sent Moses to help them get their freedom from the king of Egypt, they were happy and thanked God for remembering them. But then things didn't go as they expected! The king would not give them their freedom. Instead,

Read and Share Together

What made the Israelites unhappy?
What did the Israelites not understand?

the king made them work harder! Now they even had to find their own straw to make bricks. That must have made the Israelites grumpy and unhappy with God and Moses. The Israelites didn't understand that this was all part of God's plan to free them.

Prayer

Dear Lord, please help me not to complain or whine. Help me be happy and cheerful with a heart full of joy. Amen.

THE FIRST PLAGUES OF EGYPT

Exodus 7:14–9:7

God said to Moses, "Go meet the king at the river. Tell him to let My people go, or I will turn this river into blood." Of course, the king said no. So Moses' brother, Aaron, hit the water with his walking stick, and the river turned to blood. It smelled awful, and there was no water for the people to drink. Moses asked the king again to set God's people free. The king said no. So God sent

Read and Share Together

What did Moses ask the king?
What plagues did God send to Egypt?

frogs. Not just one or two, but more than anyone could count! The frogs went in the houses, in the beds, in the food, and in the ovens. The frogs were icky, and they were everywhere. The king still said no. Then God sent little bitty gnats that crawled all over the people. Next God sent millions of flies. They were everywhere. Cows got sick and died.

Prayer

Dear Lord, help me always to obey You when You ask me to do something for You. Amen.

A DRY PATH

Exodus 14:5–31

Moses led God's people out of Egypt and right to the banks of a huge sea called the Red Sea. There was no way to cross to the other side of the sea. And to make matters worse, the king of Egypt had changed his mind and sent his army to capture them. God's people thought they were trapped. But God was with them. God moved a tall cloud behind them to hide them from the Egyptians. He told Moses to raise his hand over the sea. God

Read and Share Together

What did God put behind the Israelites to
hide them from the Egyptians?
What did God do to the sea?

sent a wind that pushed the seawater apart and made a path right through the middle. And guess what? That path was dry. The people didn't even get their sandals muddy as they walked safely across to the other side. Only God can do a miracle like that! And did you know that when the Egyptian army tried to use the path, the water came back together! And that was the end of the king's army.

Prayer

Dear Lord, You helped Your people cross the Red Sea. I know You can take care of me too. Thank You for loving me. Amen.

THE TEN COMMANDMENTS

Exodus 20:2–17; 24:12–18; 31:18

After helping the Israelites escape Egypt, God led His people through the desert. God loved them. He made sure they had plenty of food and water. One day God called Moses to the top of a mountain to talk. That's when God gave Moses the Ten Commandments—ten rules—so that God's people would know how He wanted them to live. God wrote the rules on stone with His own finger.

Read and Share Together

What did God use to write the Ten Commandments on stone? Why did God give His people rules?

The Ten Commandments

1. God is the only true God. Love and worship only Him.
2. Do not worship or serve any other god or idol.
3. Do not use God's name thoughtlessly.
4. Keep the Sabbath day holy.
5. Honor your father and your mother.
6. Do not murder anyone.
7. Husbands and wives must be faithful to each other.
8. Do not steal.
9. Do not tell lies.
10. Do not wish for someone else's things.

Prayer

Dear Lord, thank You for the Bible. Help me
always to live by Your rules. Amen.

TWELVE MEN EXPLORE

Numbers 13:1–14:35

One day Moses sent twelve men to explore the land God was going to give His people. The land had lots of good food, but it also had large walls and people who were like giants. When the twelve men came back, ten of them said, "We can't go in and take over the land." They were afraid to trust God and try something new. Two men, Joshua and Caleb, said, "Don't worry. God is with us, and He is stronger than any giants." But the people were still afraid to go

Read and Share Together

How many of the twelve men wanted to try something new?
What happened because the people did not believe
God could help them enter the new land?

into the new land. Because the people didn't trust God to help them, they had to wander in the desert for forty years.

Prayer

Dear Lord, help me to be courageous and remember You are always with me. Amen.

THE WALLS OF JERICHO

Joshua 6

God wanted His people to capture the city of Jericho. Now Jericho was a city surrounded by huge walls. The people of Jericho closed the big heavy gates in the wall and guarded them so no one could go in or out of the city. Joshua was the leader of God's people. God told Joshua to tell the people to march

Read and Share Together

What did God ask His people to do at the walls of Jericho?
What happened when the people trusted
God and did as He said?

around the city of Jericho once a day for six days. The priests were to march in front of the Holy Box with some soldiers in front of them and other soldiers behind the Holy Box. Then on the seventh day, He wanted them to march around the city seven times. And that's not all. God said the priests were to blow their horns and the people were to give a loud shout, and then the walls would fall down. This may have seemed like a strange way to knock down the city walls, but the people trusted God and did exactly what He asked them to do, and the walls fell down.

Prayer

Dear Lord, help me always to believe You and trust Your Word even when I don't understand it. Amen.

THE SUN STANDS STILL

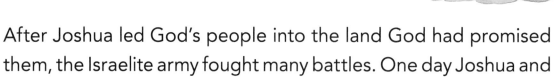

Joshua 10:1–14

After Joshua led God's people into the land God had promised them, the Israelite army fought many battles. One day Joshua and his army had been fighting hard, but the battle was not finished.

Read and Share Together

Is there anything too hard for God?
Why did Joshua need God's help?

Joshua and his army had not won—not yet. They needed more time. Joshua needed God's help and said, "Sun, stand still. . . . Moon, stand still. . . ." And the sun and moon "stopped" until Joshua and his army had won the battle. That's what God did for His people.

Prayer

Dear Lord, thank You for always being there to help me when I need You. I know You can do anything. Amen.

DEBORAH

Judges 4:1–16

When the people got settled in their new land, called the Promised Land, God gave them leaders to help them. One of them was a woman named Deborah. Deborah was called one of the great judges of Israel. People came to her under a tree so that she could

Read and Share Together

Who was Deborah?
How did Deborah help Israel?

settle their arguments. When it came time for her general Barak to go into battle, Barak did not want to go without Deborah. So she went with him, and they were victorious. Deborah was a brave woman who could win against Israel's enemies. God was on her side.

Prayer

Dear Lord, thank You for sending brave, strong, and smart leaders to help us. Amen.

GIDEON

Judges 6:11–24; 6:33–7:8; 7:16–22

Gideon was a warrior God chose to save the people of Israel from their enemy, the Midianites. God sent an angel to tell Gideon what was going to happen and what God wanted him to do. Gideon was pretty sure God had the wrong man because Gideon was the least important member of his family. Gideon

Read and Share Together

What job did God choose Gideon to do?

What did the enemy do?

was scared. But God told Gideon He would be with him. So Gideon got a big army together. "Too many," said God. Gideon sent thousands of soldiers home. "Too many still," said God, until there were only three hundred men. Then Gideon gave each man a trumpet and a jar with a burning torch inside each jar. Gideon and his men quietly went to the edge of the camp where the enemy was sleeping. His men blew their trumpets, broke the jars, let their torches shine, and shouted, "For the Lord and for Gideon!" It scared the enemy so much they began to fight each other and run away. Gideon won the battle! Hooray, Gideon! Hooray, God!

Prayer

Dear Lord, thank You for giving me victory over sin. And help me remember to ask for Your help when I have a problem. Amen.

SAMSON

Judges 13:1–5, 24–25

One of the leaders of God's people was chosen before he was born. An angel told the mother, "You will have a son! But you must never cut his hair. His long hair will show that he's a Nazirite—someone who has work to do for God." This baby grew up to be

Read and Share Together

When did God choose Samson to be a leader?
Who made Samson strong?

very strong. His name was Samson, and he always won against his enemies.

Prayer

Dear Lord, thank You for all the many strengths You have given us so that we can help one another. Amen.

RUTH AND NAOMI

Ruth 1

Ruth and Naomi were widows. That means their husbands had died. Ruth had been married to Naomi's son. One day Naomi decided to go back to the land from which her family had come. Ruth decided to go with her. Naomi thought Ruth might miss her

Read and Share Together

Whom was Ruth married to?

Who traveled with Naomi to her homeland?

family and friends. She told Ruth not to come with her. But Ruth said, "Don't ask me to leave you!" And so they went together.

Prayer

Dear Lord, thank You for sending us family and friends who stay with us no matter what happens. Amen.

RUTH AND BOAZ

Ruth 2–4

Ruth and Naomi were very poor. They didn't have enough to eat. Naomi was too old to work, so Ruth went out to a rich man's field

Read and Share Together

What was the rich man's name?
Whom did Ruth marry?

to gather leftover grain for food. The rich man was named Boaz, and he saw Ruth. She was a beautiful young woman. "Stay here and work in my field," he told her. Naomi decided Boaz would be a good husband for Ruth. She told Ruth what she should do to see if Boaz wanted to marry her. Ruth did exactly what Naomi said. Boaz liked Ruth and wanted to marry her. So they were married and had a little boy. That made all of them happy.

Prayer

Dear Lord, thank You for blessing us with happiness and with the gift of family. Amen.

HANNAH'S PRAYER

1 Samuel 1:1–2:2; 2:18–21

Hannah had no children, and that made her very sad. One day she went to God's Holy Tent, where she asked God to give her a baby son. Eli, the priest, saw her praying. Hannah told him she was very sad and talking to God about her troubles. Hannah promised that if God gave her a son, he would work for God all his life. God answered Hannah's prayer. She named her son

Read and Share Together

Why was Hannah sad?
What did Hannah pray for?

Samuel because Samuel sounds like the Hebrew word for "God heard." Hannah kept her promise, and Samuel worked for God all his life.

Prayer

Dear Lord, thank You for hearing all of our prayers. Amen.

SAMUEL LISTENS

1 Samuel 3:1–14

Samuel was a boy who lived in God's Holy Tent. His job was to help Eli, the priest. One night Samuel was asleep when he heard someone call his name. He thought it was Eli. He got up and ran

Read and Share Together

Who did Samuel think called him in the night?
What happened the fourth time Samuel
heard someone call his name?

to Eli's bed. "I didn't call you," Eli said. "Go back to bed." So Samuel did. Soon he heard the voice again. Samuel ran to Eli's bed again. After this happened three times, Eli knew God was calling Samuel. Eli said, "If you hear the voice again, Samuel, say, 'Speak, Lord. I am listening.'" And that is what Samuel did.

Prayer

Dear Lord, teach me to be quiet and listen to what You have to tell me as I read the Bible and pray. Amen.

DAVID THE SHEPHERD

1 Samuel 16:11; Psalm 23

David was a shepherd. It was his job to protect and care for sheep. When he was with the sheep, he made up songs and sang them to God. One of those songs says: "The Lord is my

Read and Share Together

What was David's job?
What did David do while he
watched the sheep?

shepherd. I have everything that I need." As David watched the sheep, he became close friends with God.

Prayer

Dear Lord, I want to spend time with You every day, just like David did because I want to be close friends with You. Amen.

DAVID AND GOLIATH

1 Samuel 17

David was a shepherd. His job was to look after his father's sheep. Some people may have thought he was just "the little guy." One day his dad sent him to take some food to his brothers who were soldiers in a war. When David got to the battle line, he couldn't believe his eyes! All the soldiers were afraid of a giant named Goliath who was yelling across the valley for God's people to send a warrior out to fight him. No one would go. Then David said, "I'll go!" "No, no!" the king said. But David was full of the courage God had given him. "God will win this battle for me," he said. David gathered five smooth stones and placed them in

Read and Share Together

Whom were the soldiers afraid of?
How did God help David win the battle?

his pouch. Then with his slingshot in one hand, off he went to fight the giant. The giant was disgusted when he saw that David was just a boy. David put a stone in the slingshot and whirled it around. The stone flew toward the giant and hit him in the head. The giant toppled to the ground. God had given David the courage to fight Goliath and win the battle.

Prayer

Dear Lord, I really want to be brave, but sometimes I feel scared. It's hard to try something new. Help me to have courage. Amen.

DAVID AND JONATHAN

1 Samuel 18:1–16; 20

David and Jonathan were best friends. Jonathan's father, Saul, was king of Israel. Prince Jonathan would have been the next king, but God had chosen David instead. The people loved David. That made King Saul angry and jealous. He was afraid of David and wanted to kill him. Jonathan heard about his father's plan and warned David. Then he helped David run far away where no one could hurt him. Jonathan even gave David his coat to wear.

Read and Share Together

Who was Jonathan's best friend?
Why was King Saul angry and jealous?

Prayer

Dear Lord, bless my friends and help us be true
friends like Jonathan and David. Amen.

JONATHAN'S SON

1 Samuel 31; 2 Samuel 1:1–4; 5:1–4; 9

Long ago David's best friend, Jonathan, died. After David became king, he wanted to show kindness to Jonathan by helping anyone who was still alive in Saul's family. David learned that Jonathan's son Mephibosheth (*mef-ee-bo'-sheth*) was crippled in both feet and living in Lo Debar. David was very kind to Mephibosheth. He treated Jonathan's son as if he were one of his own sons and always let him eat at his table. He also made sure that all of Jonathan's property was returned to Mephibosheth and that the land was farmed, so Mephibosheth would always have food to eat. Mephibosheth lived in Jerusalem, and David took care of him his whole life. David was kind.

Read and Share Together

Who is Mephibosheth?
How did David show kindness
to Mephibosheth?

Prayer

Dear Lord, I want to be a kind child and think of others first. Please help me use good manners. Amen.

ELIJAH RUNS AWAY FROM KING AHAB

1 Kings 17:1–16

Times were hard in Israel. The people had not been faithful to God, and He was not sending them rain. So God put His prophet Elijah near a stream where he would have water to drink and where birds fed him bread and meat. But after a while the stream dried up. Then God told Elijah to go to a certain woman

Read and Share Together

What did God tell Elijah to do?
What did God provide for the
woman, her son, and Elijah?

and ask her for food. Elijah went and asked. The woman said she only had enough flour and oil for one more meal for her son and herself, and then they would die of hunger. Elijah told her to cook for him first and she would be all right. Because she had a sharing heart, she did what Elijah asked and cooked him a piece of bread. Guess what? God made her food last so that the woman, her son, and Elijah would eat until once again there was food in the land.

Prayer

Dear Lord, help me learn to share with
others as You want me to. Amen.

FIRE FROM HEAVEN

1 Kings 18:1, 15–46

After about three years with no rain, the people of Israel were desperate for water. So all 450 prophets who prayed to the false god called Baal met Elijah—a prophet of the only real God—on a mountaintop. The group of prophets built an altar to Baal, placed wood on it, and then placed an offering of meat on top of the wood. Elijah did the same, but his altar was to God. The prophets yelled and screamed from morning until evening as they begged Baal to answer them and send fire. No answer came. No fire came. (This is because Baal is not a god. There is only one God. Do you know who it is?) Now it was Elijah's turn. He had people pour water on the wood and the offering of

Read and Share Together

How long had the people of Israel been without rain?
What did Elijah do when it was his turn?

meat until the altar was soaked. The people knew it was too wet for a fire to light. Next Elijah asked the real God to answer by sending fire to burn the wet offering! Just like that, God sent fire that burned up the entire altar. Wow! God had answered Elijah's prayer and proved that He was the real God.

Prayer

Dear Lord, I know You are a mighty God who
can do anything. That is why I pray to You.
Thank You for hearing my prayers. Amen.

CHARIOT OF FIRE

2 Kings 2:1–12

Elijah was a faithful servant of God. He stayed true to God even though he was threatened by a wicked queen and had to hide out in the desert. As he got older, Elijah continued to serve God faithfully. He trained his helper, Elisha, to do the same thing. Elisha went everywhere with Elijah until one day something amazing happened. Fiery horses and a chariot of fire came down from heaven, and— *WHOOSH!*—a whirlwind carried Elijah straight up to heaven. He

Read and Share Together

How would you describe Elijah?

Where did Elijah go in the whirlwind?

was faithful to God right to the end, and God was faithful to bring Elijah right up to heaven to be with Him forever.

Prayer

Dear Lord, I'm learning about being faithful. Help me be loyal, true, and dependable in everything I do. Amen.

ELISHA HELPS A LITTLE BOY

2 Kings 4:8–37

Elisha often stayed with a Shunammite woman, her husband, and their young son. The family had even built a special room for Elisha on the roof of their house. One day the little boy became sick when he went out in the field where his father was harvesting grain. They took the little boy home, but there was nothing anyone could do. The little boy died. The Shunammite woman placed the boy on Elisha's bed. She hurried to get Elisha to bring him to help her little boy. Elisha went with the lady back

Read and Share Together

What happened to the little boy?
What did God do when Elisha
prayed for the little boy?

to her house and prayed. Then all of a sudden, *"Achoo!"* The little boy sneezed. Then he sneezed six more times and opened his eyes. It was a miracle. God had brought the little boy back to life.

Prayer

Dear Lord, You are the One who gave me my breath and my sneezes. Thank You for my amazing body. Amen.

A FLOATING AX

2 Kings 6:1–7

Long ago work tools were made by hand, and tools were expensive and rare. One day sons of prophets were chopping down trees with heavy axes to build them a place to live. While they were working, a man gave a strong chop to a tree with an ax. When he did that, the heavy iron ax-head flew off the handle and went right into the water. It quickly sank. "Oh no,"

Read and Share Together

What happened to one man's ax while chopping down trees?
What did Elisha do?

said the man, "I borrowed that ax." He was sad. He wouldn't be able to return the ax to its owner. Elisha, the prophet, was there. He asked, "Where did it fall?" The man showed him. Elisha cut a stick and threw it into the water, and the heavy iron ax-head floated to the surface. The man who lost it picked it up. It was a miracle.

Prayer

Dear Lord, help me take care of anything I borrow from others as if it were my own. I want to take good care of everything I use. Thank You, Lord. Amen.

BEAUTIFUL QUEEN ESTHER

Esther 1–9

Over and over God had warned His people not to worship idols. They didn't listen. So finally God let an enemy capture His people and take them from the land He had given them. Years later Esther was an ordinary girl living in Persia. Then God chose her for an extraordinary job. First she became queen of the land. But after she was queen, one of the king's men wanted to do away with all God's people. Esther's cousin Mordecai came to her. He knew that God could use Esther

---

Read and Share Together

Where did Esther live?
What did God choose her to do?

to save God's people. He told her, "It could be that God has made you queen for just this time." What Esther did next was very courageous. Even though the king could have killed her, she went to the king and asked him to save her people. The king did what she asked. Yay, Esther!

Prayer

Dear Lord, help me to think of things I
can do to be Your helper. Amen.

A TIME FOR EVERYTHING

Ecclesiastes 3:1–8

A wise man said in the Bible that there is a right time for everything in life. Some things we can't choose, such as when to be born. But other things we can choose, such as

Read and Share Together

What does the Bible say about the time for things?
What kind of choices does God want us to make?

when to be silent and when to speak or when to hug and when not to hug or when to be happy and when to be sad. God wants us to make good choices about our time and to let Him take care of those things we can't make happen or fix or change. He is in control of everything.

Prayer

Dear Lord, please help my family and me to make good choices about what we are doing. Amen.

THREE BRAVE MEN

Daniel 3

God's people had been captured and taken away to the country of Babylon. The king of that country was Nebuchadnezzar. Three of these young men—Shadrach, Meshach, and Abednego—worked for King Nebuchadnezzar. But when the king wanted them to bow and worship a golden idol, they wouldn't do it. So the king told his soldiers to put all three men into a red-hot furnace. Guess what? The men in the furnace didn't burn up. God sent someone to protect them in the furnace. The king

Read and Share Together

What did the king want the three men to do?
What did the king see in the furnace?

was surprised when he saw four people walking around. He told Shadrach, Meshach, and Abednego to come out of the furnace. Then the king made a new law. It said that no one could say anything bad about the God of these men.

Prayer

Dear Lord, please help me always to be strong and to worship only You all the days of my life. Amen.

DANIEL AND THE LIONS' DEN

Daniel 6:11–28

Daniel was a man who loved God with all his heart. He prayed to God three times a day. The king was planning to put Daniel in charge of the whole kingdom. This made some leaders jealous, and they tricked the king into throwing Daniel into a hungry

Read and Share Together

What happened to Daniel?

Whom did God send to help Daniel?

lions' den. But God sent His angel to take care of Daniel. The angel closed the lions' jaws so they couldn't bite Daniel. In the morning, the king had Daniel removed from the lions' den. Daniel was not hurt at all, because he had trusted in God.

Prayer

Dear Lord, thank You for sending angels to watch over me. Even though I may not see them, I know they are there because Your Word tells me so. Amen.

INSIDE A BIG FISH

Jonah 1–3

God told Jonah to go to Nineveh and preach to the people. But Jonah didn't like those people, so he disobeyed God and got on a ship going the opposite direction from Nineveh. At sea, a terrible storm was about to sink the ship. Everyone was afraid. Jonah told the sailors to throw him overboard, and the

Read and Share Together

Why did Jonah disobey God?
What made Jonah change his mind about obeying God?

storm would stop. That's what they did, and the storm did stop! A large fish quickly swallowed Jonah. God let Jonah stay in the belly of that stinky old fish for three days, until Jonah prayed to Him saying he would obey. Then that fish spit Jonah up on dry land. And Jonah went straight to Nineveh and preached to the people.

Prayer

Dear Lord, help me to obey—even
when I don't want to. Amen.

AN ANGEL'S MESSAGE

Luke 1:5–20

A priest named Zechariah went to God's house to burn an incense offering. As soon as he was inside, the angel Gabriel appeared. "Zechariah, you and your wife, Elizabeth, will have a son. You will name him John," Gabriel said. Zechariah didn't

Read and Share Together

Who was Zechariah's wife?
What did the angel tell Zechariah?

believe it was possible for Elizabeth and him to have a son. They were too old. "Because you don't believe me, Zechariah, you will not be able to talk until the baby is born," Gabriel said.

Prayer

Dear Lord, thank You for blessing us and for teaching us the best way to obey You. Amen.

A BABY NAMED JOHN

Luke 1:57–66

Just as the angel Gabriel had said, a baby boy was born to Zechariah and his wife, Elizabeth. Their friends were very happy

Read and Share Together

What was the name of Elizabeth and Zechariah's baby?
What happened when Zechariah wrote down his son's name?

for them. "Name him Zechariah after his father," they said. Zechariah still couldn't talk, so he wrote down, "His name is John." As soon as Zechariah wrote that, he could talk again.

Prayer

Dear Lord, thank You for Your forgiveness. Amen.

MARY'S BIG SURPRISE

Luke 1:26–38

Not long after his visit to Zechariah, the angel Gabriel went to see a young woman named Mary. She was a cousin to Elizabeth, Zechariah's wife. Mary lived in Nazareth and was engaged to marry Joseph, the carpenter. "Don't be afraid, Mary," the angel said. "God is pleased with you. You will have a baby and will

Read and Share Together

Who visited Mary?

What did Gabriel tell Mary?

name Him Jesus. He will be called the Son of God." This was a big surprise to Mary.

Prayer

Dear Lord, thank You for sending Your
Son, Jesus, to earth. Amen.

JOSEPH MARRIES MARY

Matthew 1:18–25

When Joseph heard the news that Mary was going to have a baby, he didn't know what to think. He wasn't married to her yet. God loved Joseph and wanted him to understand that the baby was from God and everything was going to be all right. So

Read and Share Together

Whom did God send to Joseph?

What did the angel tell Joseph to name the baby?

God sent an angel to talk to Joseph in a dream. This angel told Joseph, "Name the baby Jesus. He will save people from their sins." When Joseph heard God's plan, he married Mary.

Prayer

Dear Lord, thank You for caring about how we feel and for helping us to feel better. Amen.

GOD'S BABY SON

Luke 2:1–7

The ruler of the land, Augustus Caesar, made a new law to count all the people. Everyone had to register in his hometown. So Joseph and Mary went to Joseph's hometown, Bethlehem. The town was full of people. There was no place for Mary and Joseph to sleep. Finally, Joseph found a place for them where

Read and Share Together

Where was Joseph's hometown?
Where was God's Son born?

the animals were kept. And that's where God's baby Son was born. His first bed was on the hay in the box where the animals were fed.

SOME SLEEPY SHEPHERDS

Luke 2:8–12

That night, out in the fields, sleepy shepherds were taking care of their sheep. Suddenly an angel appeared in the sky. The angel's light was so bright, it hurt their eyes. "Don't be afraid," the angel said. "I have good news for you. A baby was born in Bethlehem tonight. He is your Savior. You will find Him lying in a feeding box."

Read and Share Together

What were the shepherds doing?
Who appeared to the shepherds?

Prayer

Dear Lord, thank You for giving us the good news about Your Son so that we can share the news with others. Amen.

WHAT THE SHEPHERDS SAW

Luke 2:13–20

Then the whole sky filled up with so many angels no one could count them all. They sang, "Glory to God in heaven!" And then, when the song was over, the angels disappeared. The

Read and Share Together

What did the angels sing?
What did the shepherds do?

shepherds hurried to Bethlehem. They found Mary and Joseph and saw the baby Jesus lying in the hay in the feeding box. The shepherds told them everything the angels had said about the child.

Prayer

Dear Lord, thank You for showing us examples for how we should praise You. We can sing glory to You in heaven just like the angels do. Amen.

GIFTS FOR BABY JESUS

Matthew 2:1–12

Soon many of the people who came to register in Bethlehem went home. Mary and Joseph moved into a house. One day they

Read and Share Together

Who visited Mary and Joseph?
What did the visitors bring to
Mary, Joseph, and Jesus?

had visitors who came from far away in the East. These visitors were wise men. They had followed a bright star to find little Jesus. They bowed down and worshipped God's only Son and gave Him expensive presents of gold, frankincense, and myrrh.

Prayer

Dear Lord, thank You for guiding the wise men and me to Your Son, Jesus. Amen.

HOME AT LAST

Matthew 2:13–15, 19–23

After the wise men left, God sent another angel to Joseph in a dream. "Take the child and Mary and go to Egypt," the angel said. "King Herod wants to kill Jesus. Stay in Egypt until I tell you it's safe to come home." It was still night, but Joseph got up out of bed and took Mary and Jesus and headed for Egypt. Mary, Joseph, and Jesus stayed in Egypt until God sent another angel to Joseph in a dream. "Get up and take Mary and Jesus and go

Read and Share Together

Where did the angel tell Joseph to take Mary and Jesus?
Where did Joseph, Mary, and Jesus return to?

home," said the angel. King Herod had died. He could never hurt them again. God and His angels had kept Mary, Joseph, and Jesus safe. So with happy hearts, they went home to live in Nazareth.

Prayer

Dear Lord, thank You for watching over me and guiding me through the good days and the bad days. I feel safe knowing You care for me. Amen.

JESUS WITH THE TEMPLE TEACHERS

Luke 2:41–52

When Jesus was twelve years old, He went with His parents to the temple in Jerusalem. Soon it was time to go home to Nazareth. Everyone packed up and left. At first Mary and Joseph thought Jesus was traveling with some of their family and friends. When they realized Jesus wasn't in the group, they went back to Jerusalem, where they found Jesus talking with some religious

Read and Share Together

What was Jesus doing in the temple?
How did Jesus honor His parents?

teachers in the temple just as if He were one of them. When Mary and Joseph told Jesus it was time to go, He honored them by respectfully doing what they asked. He left the teachers and went home with Mary and Joseph. There He continued to learn and grow, to obey His parents, and to please God in all that He did.

Prayer

Dear Lord, please help me be the child You want
me to be and honor my parents. Amen.

JOHN BAPTIZES JESUS

Matthew 3; Mark 1:4–11

Jesus' cousin, John, became a preacher when he grew up. He lived in the desert and wore rough clothes and ate locusts and honey. (Locusts were like grasshoppers.) John told the people to change their hearts and lives and ask forgiveness for their wrongs because Jesus was coming soon. One day when Jesus was grown up, too, He came to the place where John was preaching and baptizing people. Jesus asked John to baptize Him in the river. At first John didn't want to baptize Jesus. He thought Jesus should be the one to baptize him. But when Jesus said it needed to be this way, John obeyed and took Jesus into

Read and Share Together

Who was John?
What did Jesus ask John
to do for Him?

the river and baptized Him. As Jesus came up out of the water, God's Spirit, like a dove, came down to Him from heaven. God spoke and said, "This is My Son, and I love Him. I am very pleased with Him."

Prayer

Dear Lord, thank You for sending us people who help us to understand that we can be washed clean of sin. Amen.

JESUS TEMPTED BY SATAN

Matthew 4:1–11

When Jesus was tempted, He was out in the desert all alone. Jesus was very hungry and tired when Satan came to tempt Him to do some things that were wrong. First Satan told Jesus to "turn these rocks into bread." But Jesus had studied God's Word, so He remembered what He had learned from the Scriptures. He said, "A person doesn't live just by eating bread. A person lives by doing everything the Lord says." "Jump down from the top of the temple. God's angels will catch you," said Satan. Jesus answered, "The Scriptures also say, 'Do

Read and Share Together

How was Jesus feeling when Satan came to Him?
Did Jesus do the right or the wrong thing?

not test God.'" Then Satan took Jesus to the top of a tall mountain and showed Him all the kingdoms of the world. "Bow down and give honor to me, and I will give you all these things," said Satan. But Jesus said, "Go away from Me! It is written in the Scriptures, 'You must worship only the Lord God.'" And Satan left.

Prayer

Dear Lord, sometimes it is hard to do what is right. Please help me say no to temptation and to do the right thing. Amen.

JESUS HEALS A SICK BOY

John 4:46–53

One day at exactly one o'clock in the afternoon, an important man in the government begged Jesus to come heal his son. The boy was very, very sick and in a different town. Jesus knew He didn't need to go there. He told the father, "Go home. Your son will live." The man believed Jesus and went home. On the man's way home, his servants met him and told him his son was well. The father asked what time

Read and Share Together

What did Jesus do when the man
asked Him to heal his son?
Who believed in Jesus?

his son began to get well. The servants said, "Your son's fever went away at one o'clock yesterday." The father knew that was the exact time Jesus had said, "Your son will live." Now not only did the man believe in Jesus, all the people in his house believed in Jesus too.

Prayer

Dear Lord, help me eat right and sleep well
to help my body be healthy. Amen.

A LITTLE BOY HELPS JESUS

John 6:1–14; Matthew 14:13–21

One day a crowd of people followed Jesus to see His miracles and hear Him teach about God's love. By the time they reached Jesus, it was late in the day, and there were more than five thousand hungry people. But there was no food, except for five small loaves of bread and two small fish that a boy had brought with him. The boy gave his bread and fish to Jesus' helpers. Jesus thanked God for the boy's food and gave everyone there

Read and Share Together

What was in the boy's lunch?
What did Jesus do?

as much to eat as they wanted. It was a miracle. There were even twelve baskets of food left over!

Prayer

Dear Lord, I want to help others. Please show
me ways that I can be helpful. Amen.

JESUS WALKS ON THE WATER

Mark 6:45–53

One day Jesus asked His helpers to go to a town across the lake. He said He would join them later. The men did as Jesus asked and got into a boat and set out across the lake. A strong wind came up. The wind blew fiercely. The men were very afraid! They rowed harder and harder toward the shore, but the wind kept

Read and Share Together

What made Jesus' helpers afraid?
What did Jesus do?

pushing them back into the lake. Then they saw something that scared them even more. A man was walking on the water toward them! Then the man called out, "Don't be afraid." And they realized it was Jesus walking toward them. Jesus got into their boat, and suddenly the wind became calm. The helpers were amazed. Everything was all right because Jesus was with them.

Prayer

Dear Lord, sometimes I am afraid. Help me know that You are always with me and to ask for Your help when I'm afraid. Amen.

JESUS LOVES CHILDREN

Matthew 19:13–15; Mark 10:13–16;
Luke 18:15–17

So many people wanted to see Jesus that they were squishing Him. There were sick people and sad people and well people and happy people, and there were people who brought their children to meet Jesus. "No children," Jesus' helpers said to the people. "Jesus doesn't have time for them." Jesus heard what His helpers said. He stopped them right there. "Let the little children come to Me," Jesus said, and He began to bless the children. Children are impor- tant to God. Children are important to Jesus. He loves them. He loves you!

Read and Share Together

Why did Jesus' helpers want to send the children away?
What did Jesus say to His helpers?

Prayer

Dear Lord, thank You for loving me so
much. I love You too. Amen.

A VERY SHORT MAN

Luke 19:1–10

Everywhere Jesus went, there were crowds of people. In one crowd there was a very short man named Zacchaeus. He wanted to see Jesus, but he couldn't see over the crowd. So he climbed a tree. Jesus said, "Zacchaeus, come down so we can go to your house today." Zacchaeus hurried down and

Read and Share Together

Who climbed a tree to see Jesus?
What did Zacchaeus tell Jesus he would do?

took Jesus to his home. Zacchaeus wanted to do good things. He told Jesus that he'd give half of his money to the poor.

Prayer

Dear Lord, thank You for showing me how I can be a great person by loving You and treating people fairly. Amen.

A COIN IN A FISH

Matthew 17:24–27

When Jesus lived on earth, He paid taxes, just as people do today. One day His friend Peter came to tell Jesus they didn't have any money to pay their taxes. That didn't bother Jesus at all. "Go fishing, Peter. You will catch a fish, and there will be a coin in its mouth. Use that to pay our taxes." Peter had been fishing all his life, and surely he had never once found a coin in a fish's mouth. But he trusted Jesus. Soon Peter caught a fish, and it had a coin in its mouth. Peter used the money to pay their taxes.

Read and Share Together

What did Jesus and Peter need?
What big surprise did Peter get
when he caught a fish?

Prayer

Dear Lord, thank You for sharing Your love with me
and giving me what I need. I love You. Amen.

A BLIND MAN SEES AGAIN

Mark 10:46–52

Jesus can do anything! He can heal sick people, and He can make blind people able to see again. One day a crowd of people was following Jesus. A blind man, who was sitting by the road, kept calling out, "Jesus, please help me!" He was so loud that some of the crowd told him to be quiet. Jesus ignored the crowd. He asked the blind man, "What would you like Me to do for you?" The blind man said, "I want to see." Jesus said, "You are healed because you believe." Now the man could see.

Read and Share Together

What did Jesus ask the blind man?
What did Jesus do for the blind man?

Prayer

Dear Lord, please help those who cannot see. Amen.

A VERY POOR WOMAN

Mark 12:41–44

Jesus watched as people put their money in an offering box at the temple. The rich people were giving a lot of money. But then, from the back of the crowd came a very poor woman. She dropped her two copper coins into the box. When Jesus saw

Read and Share Together

Who gave all she had?
What did Jesus say about her gift?

her, He said to His followers, "This woman gave more than the rich people with many coins. She gave all the money she had."

Prayer

Dear Lord, help me to give with a happy heart. Thank You for blessing me in so many ways. Amen.

JESUS STOPS A STORM

Mark 4:35–41

One day after Jesus had been teaching all day long, He and His friends got into a boat to go across the lake. Jesus was so tired He fell asleep. Before His friends could row across the lake, up came a strong storm. The wind began to whip around. Waves splashed high against the boat and began to fill it with water.

Read and Share Together

What did Jesus do when He got into the boat?
What did Jesus say to the storm?

It was a scary time. Finally, Jesus' friends woke Him up. They were afraid. "Help us, or we'll drown!" they said. Jesus stood up, and instead of grabbing an oar to help row, He spoke to the storm. "Quiet! Be still!" Jesus said. The wind stopped. The waves calmed down, and everyone was safe. Jesus is so mighty the wind and waves obey Him!

Prayer

Dear Lord, You are so mighty You can do anything. Thank You for being with me all the time—in stormy and sunny weather. Amen.

ONE LOST SHEEP

Luke 15:3–7

Jesus told a story about a shepherd who had one hundred sheep. Every night when the shepherd brought his sheep home he counted them to make sure they were all there. One night after he counted ninety-nine sheep, there were no more sheep

Read and Share Together

Who is the Good Shepherd?
What did the shepherd do when he
found one sheep missing?

to count. One sheep was missing. The shepherd left his ninety-nine sheep safe at home and went right out to find the one lost sheep. He looked high. He looked low. He looked everywhere. And finally he found the sheep. The happy shepherd put the sheep on his shoulders—that's the way shepherds used to carry their sheep—and brought it home. The shepherd was so happy that he had a party with his friends to celebrate finding his lost sheep.

Prayer

Dear Lord, I'm so glad You care about me. Thank You for coming to search for me when I wander off in my heart and forget to follow You. Help me to love and obey You. Amen.

GOING HOME TO FATHER

Luke 15:11–24

There was a man who had two sons. The younger son decided he wanted the money that would be his when his father died while his father was still alive. His father gave him the money. The son went off to another country and spent all his money on

Read and Share Together

What happened to the younger son's money?
When the younger son came home, what did his father do?

foolish things. After his money was gone, the son was hungry and alone. He got a job feeding pigs, and he was so hungry he even thought about eating the pigs' food. Then he realized that his father's servants had more food than he had. He decided to go home, tell his father he was sorry, and ask if he could just be a servant. And that's what he did. To his surprise, when he went home, his father gave him a big hug and forgave him for all he had done.

Prayer

Dear Lord, I ask You to forgive me for the wrongs I have done. Help me to do what is right. Amen.

JESUS' BEST FRIENDS

Luke 10:38–42

One day Jesus went to visit some best friends named Mary, Martha, and Lazarus. Martha was busy getting the meal ready. Mary was sitting and listening to Jesus talk. Martha became

Read and Share Together

Why was Martha angry?
What did Jesus tell her?

angry and complained, "Jesus, don't You care that Mary left me to do all this work alone? Tell her to help me." Jesus said, "What Mary is learning from Me can never be taken away from her."

Prayer

Dear Lord, what I learn from You can never be taken away from me. Amen.

JESUS BRINGS LAZARUS BACK TO LIFE

John 11:1–44

Jesus loved His friends Martha, Mary, and Lazarus. One day when Jesus was away, Lazarus became ill. When Jesus heard His friend was ill, Jesus waited two days to start His trip to see His friends. By the time Jesus arrived, Lazarus had been dead for four days. Lazarus' sister Mary said, "Jesus, if You had been here, my brother would not have died." Jesus was so sad, He cried. Then Jesus walked to Lazarus'

Read and Share Together

What did Jesus do when He heard
His friend Lazarus had died?
What happened next?

tomb and asked the people there to move the stone from the entrance. In a loud voice Jesus said, "Lazarus, come out!" And out of the tomb walked Lazarus, all wrapped up in burial clothes! He was alive and well.

Prayer

Dear Lord, I know it's okay to be sad sometimes.
Thank You for the happy memories I have of those
who have gone to heaven to be with You. Amen.

ONE MAN SAYS THANK YOU

Luke 17:11–19

One day Jesus was walking along a road when He saw ten men. They did not come close to Jesus because they had a skin disease called leprosy. The men called out to Jesus, "Please help us." Jesus healed all ten men. As they went on their way, the sores and bumps on their skin went away—which meant that their skin

Read and Share Together

What did the ten men ask Jesus to do?
How many men said thank you?

disease disappeared. They were well. When one of the ten men saw that his skin was healed, he turned around and hurried back to thank Jesus for healing him. But he was the only one to say thank you. He had a thankful heart.

Prayer

Dear Lord, thank You for my family. Please help me to be thankful for all of my blessings every day. Amen.

JESUS RIDES LIKE A KING

Luke 19:28–38; John 12:12–16

The first Passover happened when God's people left Egypt long ago. After that, God's people celebrated the Passover every year. One year Jesus and His closest followers went to Jerusalem to celebrate the Passover. Before they got there, Jesus said to His followers, "Go into town and find a young donkey colt. Untie it and bring it to Me. If anyone asks where you are taking it, say, 'The Master needs it.'" When the men got back with the donkey colt, they spread their coats on its back. Jesus climbed on the colt. The donkey rode through the town.

Read and Share Together

Why do you suppose the people laid down
their coats for the donkey to walk on?
Whom did they think Jesus was?

People threw their coats down for the donkey to walk on. They took palm branches and waved them in the air. "Praise God!" they shouted.

Prayer

Dear Lord, help me learn how best to praise
Your name all the days of my life. Amen.

JESUS SHOWS HOW TO SERVE

John 13:1–17

During Jesus' last days on earth, He and His closest followers had an evening meal together. It was the time of the Jewish Passover Feast. During their meal, Jesus got up from the table,

Read and Share Together

What were Jesus and His followers doing?
During dinner, what did Jesus do?

took off His coat, wrapped a towel around His waist, and poured water into a big bowl. Then He went from one of His friends to the next washing their dusty, maybe even smelly, feet. He did this to show them how to serve one another. If Jesus, their leader, could act as their servant and wash their feet, they could do things to help and serve others too.

Prayer

Dear Lord, if You can be a servant to others, so can I. Help me find ways to serve others. Amen.

THE FIRST LORD'S SUPPER

Matthew 26:26–29; 1 Corinthians 11:23–25

While Jesus and His closest followers were eating the Passover dinner, Jesus took some bread and thanked God for it. He broke the bread apart and said, "Take this bread and eat it. Do this to remember Me." Next He took a cup and said, "When you drink this juice of the grape, remember Me."

Read and Share Together

What did Jesus do with the bread and the cup?
What did Jesus want His disciples to remember?

Jesus knew this was His last meal with His followers because He was about to be killed. He wanted His followers to remember Him always.

Prayer

Dear Lord, thank You for letting us be a
part of the Lord's Supper. Amen.

A DARK DAY

Matthew 27:27–40, 45–54; Mark 15:25–27; Luke 23:44–49; Hebrews 9

Pilate's soldiers took Jesus and put a crown of thorns on His head and made fun of Him. Then they led Jesus out of the city to a place called Golgotha to be killed on a cross. At nine o'clock in the morning, the soldiers nailed Jesus to the cross. They also put two robbers beside Jesus, one on the right and one on the left. While Jesus was on the cross, the land became dark from noon until three o'clock. Then Jesus died, and there was a big earthquake. When the earth shook, the thick curtain in the temple between the Holy Place and the Most Holy Place ripped from

Read and Share Together

When Jesus was on the cross, what happened to the light?
What did the soldiers know when Jesus died?

top to bottom. Now people could see inside the Most Holy Place. Before, only the high priest got to see inside. When the soldiers at the cross saw what happened when Jesus died, they knew He really was the Son of God!

Prayer

Dear Lord, thank You for sending Your Son to die for our sins, even though it was very sad and painful. Amen.

A BIG SURPRISE

Matthew 28:1–10; Luke 23:50–56

A rich man, named Joseph of Arimathea, had a new tomb where he had planned to be buried. He took Jesus' body from the cross and put it in his own empty tomb. Joseph and Jesus' friends wrapped His body in strips of linen and laid it carefully in the tomb. Roman soldiers came to guard the tomb. They rolled a huge stone over the door and sealed it in a way that would show if anyone tried to move the stone. The day after Jesus was buried was a holy day, so His friends had to stay home. Then very early on Sunday morning, the first day of the week, the women went back to the tomb. It was the third

Read and Share Together

Where was Jesus buried?
What did the women find when they
visited Jesus' tomb the next day?

day since Jesus died. When the women got there, they couldn't believe their eyes. The stone had been rolled away! An angel of God was sitting on the stone! The soldiers were so frightened they were like dead men.

Prayer

Dear Lord, thank You for defeating death and for raising Jesus from the dead. Praise God, the stone was rolled away! Amen.

JESUS GOES TO HEAVEN

Luke 24:13–53; Acts 1:6–11

After Jesus' death and His resurrection, He appeared to many people. He wanted them to believe He is alive. Two of Jesus' friends were walking along the road, and Jesus joined them and talked with them. Then one night Jesus appeared in a room where many of His friends were gathered. He told them to tell their family and friends and neighbors and even strangers that He is alive. Later Jesus led His followers a little way out of town. Jesus prayed for His followers, and while He was praying,

Read and Share Together

Why did Jesus appear to His friends?
What happened to Jesus after He led
His followers outside of town?

He started to rise up into heaven. Then a cloud hid Him from His followers. As everyone was standing there staring up into heaven, two angels appeared beside them and said, "Jesus has been taken away from you and into heaven. He will come back in the clouds, just like He went away."

Prayer

Dear Lord, You are almighty and wonderful. You
want the whole world to know about Your Son,
and I want to share the good news! Amen.

GOD'S SPIRIT COMES TO HELP

Acts 2:1–42

After Jesus went back to heaven, His friends and helpers were praying together in a big room. Suddenly something amazing happened. First it sounded as if a huge wind were blowing. Next flames of fire flickered over every person's head. Then

Read and Share Together

What flickered over every person's head in the big room?
Who brought a gift from God to His followers?

God's Spirit came, and everyone began to speak in different languages. This was the gift from God that Jesus had promised His followers. The day that God's Spirit came to Jesus' followers, there were people from many countries in Jerusalem. These people spoke different languages. When they heard Jesus' friends praying, they went to see what the noise was all about. They found Jesus' friends telling about the great things God had done. But they were all surprised to hear it in their own language. "What does this mean?" they asked.

Prayer

Dear Lord, You have blessed us with Your wonderful gifts. Please help me know how to use mine. Amen.

PETER IN JAIL

Acts 12:1–18

One day mean King Herod threw Peter, one of Jesus' followers, in jail. The king had sixteen soldiers guard Peter so he couldn't get away. That night an angel came into Peter's cell. "Hurry! Get up!" the angel said. "Follow me." Peter thought he must be dreaming . . . but he wasn't. The chains fell off his hands, and the angel led him past the guards. When they came to the iron gate of the prison, it swung open on its own, and Peter was free.

Read and Share Together

Who visited Peter in jail?
How did Peter escape jail?

Prayer

Dear Lord, You set Peter free from jail. Thank You
for setting us free in all kinds of ways. Amen.

NEW HEAVEN AND EARTH

John 14:1–2; Revelation 21

One day Jesus talked with His friends and followers about heaven. He said, "Don't let your hearts be troubled. Trust in God. And trust in Me. There are many rooms in My Father's house. I would not tell you this if it were not true. I am going there to prepare a place for you." God promises that

Read and Share Together

What did Jesus say He was going
to do for us in heaven?
Will we be sad in heaven?

in heaven no one will ever be sad again. No one will ever be sick again. Everything will be more wonderful than we have ever imagined. And we will be happy there forever.

Prayer

Dear Lord, thank You for Your promise of heaven. I know You have lots of things for me to do first in this life. But it's so good to know You have a place waiting for me. Amen.